D1119961

MONSTER MANIA

GHOSTS

John Malam

QEB Publishing

Illustrator: Vincent Boulanger
Editor: Amanda Askew
Designer: Matthew Kelly
Picture Researcher: Maria Joannou

Published in the United States by
QEB Publishing, Inc.
3 Wrigley, Suite A
Irvine, CA 92618

www.qed-publishing.co.uk

Library of Congress Cataloging-in-Publication Data

Malam, John, 1957-
Ghosts / John Malam.
p. cm. -- (QEB Monster mania)
Includes bibliographical references and index.
ISBN 978-1-59566-750-2 (library binding : alk. paper)
1. Ghosts--Juvenile literature. I. Title.
BF1461.M34 2011
133.1--dc22

2010008529

Printed in China

Words in **bold** can be found in the Glossary on page 31.

Acknowledgments
Alamy Images Mary Evans Picture Library 12, The Marsden Archive 21b, Pictorial
Press Ltd 30; **Bridgeman Art Library** Private Collection 4;
Corbis Jessica Rinaldi/Reuters 20, 29t; **Getty Images** Workbook Stock/Luca
Zampedri 5, Stone/Ralf Nau 8, National Geographic/Steve And Donna O'Meara
9b, Jane Sweeney/Robert Harding 16, Hulton Archive/Mills 17b, Time & Life
Pictures 21t; **Science Photo Library** Garion Hutchings 25b; **Shutterstock** Elixirpix
9t, Olly 13, R. Formidable 17t; **Topham Picturepoint** Fortean 24, 25t, AP 28,
Charles Walker 29b

CONTENTS

A WORLD OF GHOSTS

Who or what are **ghosts**? The truth is, no one knows what ghosts are, or even if they exist. However, this doesn't stop people from believing in them, and many claim to have seen ghosts. To these people, ghosts are real.

It's said that most ghosts are the **spirits** of people who have died. Instead of leaving the world of the living, they are stranded on Earth as shadowy figures that move through walls, float across the ground, and cause things to go bump in the night.

Some people believe that ghosts are friendly messengers, trying to contact the living. Others think that ghosts are harmful, seeking revenge against those who wronged them in their human lives.

Famous ghost story

One of the most famous ghost stories ever written is *A Christmas Carol*, by Charles Dickens. The story, which came out in 1843, is about three ghosts that visit Ebenezer Scrooge on Christmas Eve to teach him about love and joy at Christmas time.

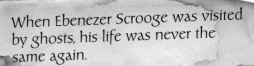

When Ebenezer Scrooge was visited by ghosts, his life was never the same again.

4

WHO'S WHO AMONG GHOSTS?

DOPPELGANGER

Doppelganger is a German word meaning "double-walker." It is the ghost of a person who is still alive and it seems to be the person's ghostly double. The double looks like the real person, except that it has a misty, see-through appearance.

A doppelganger is thought to be a sign of bad luck that means the living person is about to die.

AND THE REST...

APPARITION, SPOOK, OR PHANTOM

The common words for a ghost, something that appears out of nowhere.

POLTERGEIST

A ghost that is invisible. It draws attention to itself by throwing things and by making banging noises. *Poltergeist* is German for "noisy ghost."

ANIMAL GHOSTS

Just like people, the spirits of some dead animals are thought to remain behind as ghosts.

The GHOSTS AT THE PALACE

When English tourists Charlotte Moberly and Eleanor Jourdain visited Versailles, France, they believed they had slipped back in time. Instead of being in the year 1901, the women felt they were in 1789, and were surrounded by ghosts from the past.

After visiting the Palace of Versailles, the ladies had walked to the nearby Petit Trianon —a grand house that once belonged to Queen Marie Antoinette. They entered the yard, and that's when the **time slip** happened.

Something felt strange, as if the world was suddenly different. The air was still and heavy. They saw gardeners at work, a young woman sketching, and a man running. Everyone was dressed in unfamiliar clothes—the clothes worn by people from long ago.

This story comes from
FRANCE

After a few minutes, the heavy feeling vanished—and so did the strange figures. Charlotte and Eleanor were convinced they had seen ghosts of the people who had once lived at Versailles, and the woman seen sketching was none other than Marie Antoinette.

Charlotte and Eleanor could hardly believe their eyes—was it really the ghost of Queen Marie Antoinette?

Marie Antoinette

Marie Antoinette was born in Austria, in 1755. She became Queen of France in 1774, when her husband was crowned King Louis XVI. She was unpopular with the people of France, and during the French Revolution she was executed in 1793.

The causes of
GHOSTS

If ghosts really do exist, then something must cause them— but what? There are lots of ideas about the causes of ghosts, each trying to explain the mystery.

RESTLESS SPIRITS

Ghosts are the souls or spirits of dead people. Instead of leaving this world after death, the spirit stays behind, trapped and restless. It could be because it refuses to accept the death of its human body, to stay close to a loved one or to take revenge for something bad that has happened during the person's life.

The human body has died, and in its place remains the restless spirit of a ghost.

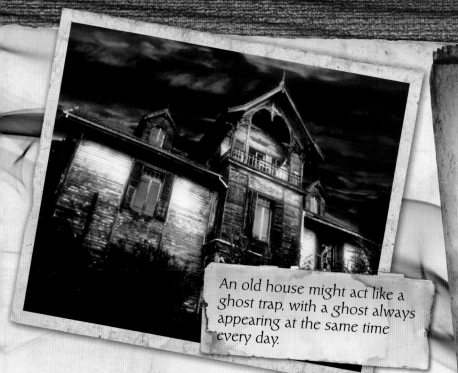

An old house might act like a ghost trap, with a ghost always appearing at the same time every day.

Out-of-body experience

Perhaps ghosts can be explained as out-of-body experiences, or OBEs. A person's spirit leaves their body while they are still alive, then travels to another place where it might be seen as a "ghost." The spirit returns to the body when its travels are over.

CYCLICAL GHOSTS

Eyewitnesses claim that some ghosts haunt particular places, often at set times. For example, an old house might have an apparition that appears in the same room and at the same time every day. These are so-called **cyclical ghosts**. They go round in cycles, repeating the same things.

DREAMS AND THOUGHT FORMS

Ghosts are usually seen at night, so perhaps they are no more than dreams. Another idea is they are "thought forms," created simply by thinking about them—the result of people's vivid imagination.

Some people believe that a ghost can be made to appear simply by the power of a person's imagination.

9

The Most Haunted House
IN ENGLAND

Borley Rectory was doomed from the day it was built in 1863, on the site of an old monastery where a nun was said to have been buried alive. A ghost hunter claimed that it was the most haunted house in England.

Reverend Henry Bull and his family moved into their new home and, to their horror, found they were not alone. They heard footsteps, knocking, and sobbing noises, and saw the shadowy figure of a nun gliding across the yard.

Reverend Bull watched as the ghost of a nun crossed the yard.

This story comes from
ENGLAND

When Harry Price found the skull fragment, he was certain he had solved the mystery of Borley Rectory.

haunted castle

Ghosts are often linked with castles. One of the world's most haunted castles is in Glamis, Scotland, U.K. It is the haunt of the ghost of Janet Douglas, who was burned at the stake in 1537. Her ghost is said to appear over the castle clock tower, glowing orange, as if it is on fire.

The Bull family moved away in 1927 and the Smith family moved in. They also heard footsteps and sobbing, and a poltergeist threw objects across the rooms. They soon left the rectory.

Next came the Foysters, and there were more scares than ever. Writing appeared on walls, and Mrs. Foyster was slapped by an invisible hand.

Harry Price, a famous ghost hunter, contacted the spirit of a dead nun, who told him the house would burn down and the bones of a nun would be found in the ruins. In 1939, Borley Rectory burned to the ground, and when Price dug under the basement floor, he found part of a human skull.

POLTERGEISTS
the noisy ghosts

If an object suddenly flew across the room, you might believe a poltergeist was to blame. These are invisible ghosts, who make their presence known by moving objects and by making noises.

WHAT IS A POLTERGEIST?

Unlike ghosts that can be seen, which might be the spirits of dead people, poltergeists are thought to be a type of energy. Whatever this energy is, it seems to be attracted to a particular person, often a teenage girl.

If objects suddenly start to move around on their own, it might be the work of a poltergeist.

Out of thin air

An object that appears out of thin air, or seems to move through solid matter, is called an apport. Most are small objects, such as items of jewelry, but larger objects, such as books, are also said to have appeared from nowhere.

STRANGE HAPPENINGS

Suddenly, and without any warning, strange things happen around the teenage girl. Earthenware is thrown across the room and smashed to pieces, objects float in the air, doors and windows open and close on their own, lights switch on and off, and things just vanish and are nowhere to be found.

NOISY SPIRITS

There's more to poltergeists than just being mischievous spirits. When all is quiet, they disturb the peace with sudden, loud bangs, tapping and scratching on walls, and rattling windows. Footsteps thud loudly across the room, bad smells fill the air and small fires break out.

Unexplained fires, especially small ones, have been blamed on poltergeists.

The Baltimore POLTERGEIST

For three weeks in 1960, a house in Baltimore was disturbed by strange goings-on. Was it a poltergeist or just a faulty boiler?

It started when the Jones family was having their evening meal. Suddenly, a vase exploded into tiny pieces, and then another, and another, until fifteen lay broken on the floor.

Ted seemed to be at the center of the poltergeist activity—but why?

Over the next few days, pictures popped off their hooks and crashed to the ground, and a sugar bowl floated through the air, then spilled sugar onto a table.

A ghost hunter visited the family. He noticed that seventeen-year-old Ted's passion for writing was ignored. So Ted's feelings of frustration built up inside him until they turned into an energy force—a force that had the power to move objects. This, said the ghost hunter, accounted for the poltergeist activity.

A ghost hunter thought Ted could make objects move simply by thinking about them.

A plumber said it was because air pressure had built up inside the house from the boiler. He told the Joneses to open the windows, so that the pressure inside the house would be the same as outside. They did as they were told, and the weird things stopped. In the Jones' minds, the plumber had solved the mystery.

Mind control —fact or fiction?

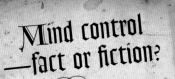

The power to move objects by thought alone is called **psychokinesis**, or PK. Many people have said they can do this, especially those who claim they can make contact with spirits. Some people think it's no more than stage magic, designed to trick people.

This story comes from
Maryland

15

TALKING TO GHOSTS

If ghosts are real, perhaps it's because they want to make contact with the living. This idea has been around for thousands of years, and many people claim to have talked to them.

TALKING TO SPIRITS

In tribal communities, people with this gift are shamans, medicine men, and wise women. Elsewhere they are known as **psychics**, mystics and, most of all, **mediums**. Ghost talkers usually enter into trances to contact the spirit world. They act as go-betweens, linking the world of the living with the world of the dead.

Shamans are believed to have the power to talk to the dead.

The Ouija board

At a seance, a medium might use a Ouija (say: we-ja) board. The letters of the alphabet are printed on the board, and a pointer rests on top of it. A question is asked, and if a spirit answers it, the pointer moves from letter to letter, spelling out the spirit's reply.

A photograph from the 1920s showing people taking part in a séance.

SPIRIT MEETINGS

For many people, the idea of contacting the spirit of a loved one is irresistible. It's a chance to ask questions and, hopefully, receive answers. Mediums hold a meeting to contact the spirits called a **seance**. People can ask questions, and the medium passes on the spirits' answers.

TRICKSTERS

Many mediums have been caught out as tricksters. They change the sound of their voices and only pretend to be speaking to spirits. They make up answers that people want to hear.

The Table-tapping
SISTERS

Maggie and Kate Fox from the town of Hydesville said they could talk to spirits. People flocked to their house, eager to contact their loved ones who had died. The year was 1848.

It all began when Maggie, aged 15, and Kate, aged 12, discovered that when they clapped their hands, a rapping noise answered back. It was as if the girls were being used as a channel to reach into the spirit world.

The girls' claps and the ghostly raps were used to spell out letters, which built up into words and sentences. Newspapers reported on these events, and the Fox sisters became well known. They gave public performances, where strange rapping noises were accompanied by flying objects and floating tables.

Maggie and Kate Fox caused a sensation when they said they could contact the spirit world.

The sisters carried on with their acts of spiritualism for many years. Then, in 1888, Maggie and Kate confessed that they had been pretending all along. They had made the rapping noises by cracking the joints of their toes.

This story comes from New York

Sir Arthur Conan Doyle

Arthur Conan Doyle (1859–1930) is best known as the writer of the Sherlock Holmes detective stories. He was also a big fan of spiritualism and wrote several books about the subject.

Ghosts on CAMERA

Is it possible to prove that ghosts exist? Ghost hunters think it is. They started taking cameras and other recording equipment to haunted places and have recorded some truly unusual images.

TAKING PHOTOGRAPHS

For many people, photographs of ghosts are fake. Some might have been made on purpose, to fool people. Others might be tricks of the light or shadows. Today, cameras are everywhere, which can only mean there's a greater chance of photographing something unusual—something that might just prove the existence of ghosts.

A group of ghost-hunters from Rhode Island called the Valley Rangers Paranormal Investigators, bang on a door at a cemetery to provoke the ghosts that dwell there.

RAYNHAM HALL

One of the most famous ghost photographs of all time was taken by chance. It happened in 1936, when magazine photographers took pictures inside Raynham Hall, a country house in Norfolk, England.

A photograph of the main staircase showed the ghostly figure of a woman in a wedding dress. The house is said to be haunted by Lady Dorothy Townshend, who once lived there. Her ghost, known as the Brown Lady, has been seen many times.

The Brown Lady ghost, photographed at Raynham Hall in 1936.

Raynham Hall is a country house in Norfolk, England. Its famous ghost might be of Lady Dorothy Townshend, who lived there in the early 1700s.

Ghost on the phone

The phone rings, and the voice on the other end is from someone who has died. The line is crackly as if the ghostly voice is calling from far away. Soon, the voice fades, until all that is left on the line is the empty sound of silence.

HOUSE OF HORRORS

In December 1975, George and Kathleen Lutz moved into their new house in Amityville. The year before, a family had been murdered there, and when the house was put up for sale, no one wanted it—except the Lutzes.

Within a month of moving in, the Lutzes fled the house. They said it was filled with a bad smell, slime oozed from the walls, and there were swarms of flies. Doors slammed, and footprints from an unknown creature were found in the snow. Mrs. Lutz claimed she was grabbed by unseen hands, and one night she said she floated up from her bed and turned into a wrinkled old lady.

The Lutzes told their story to a writer, and his book, *The Amityville Horror: A True Story*, became a bestseller and was made into a successful movie. The problem was, it was just that—a story.

Haunted prison

The island of Alcatraz, in San Francisco Bay was home to a famous prison. Alcatraz closed in 1963, and is now visited by tourists. Some have said they felt they were being watched, and could hear footsteps and shouting. Others claim to have seen the ghosts of prisoners passing through the walls, as if trying to escape.

When investigators looked into the story they were certain the whole thing was a **hoax**. For example, no snow had fallen on the night the Lutzes said they found the footprints. The whole thing had been made up by the Lutzes.

It might look like a scene from a horror film, but the Lutzes said that slime covered the walls of their house.

GHOSTLY LIGHTS

According to ghost hunters, ghosts don't need to appear in human shape. Balls of light known as **orbs** can be detected only by cameras that show infrared images. The light floats through the air in straight lines, as if a person is walking along.

TRICK OF THE EYE

Orbs have been photographed and filmed many times, and different ideas exist to explain them. For people who do not believe in ghosts, orbs are simply specks of dust, grains of pollen, or water droplets reflected back into the lens of the camera.

Only after this photograph was taken did people see the bright light next to the man. The question is: what is it?

ENERGY FORMS

However, for believers in ghosts, orbs are signs of something else. These people believe that orbs are forms of pure energy that are released when a person dies. The spirits of the dead use orbs to show that they are still here among the living.

Another idea says that orbs are bundles of energy from events that happened in the past, trapped in the atmosphere. The bigger the event was, the more energy would have been released.

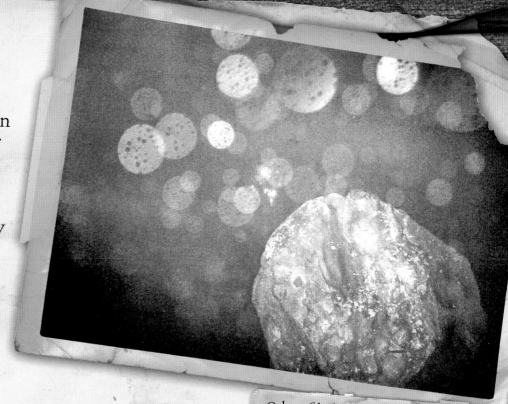

Orbs of light, photographed over the prehistoric Avebury stones in Wiltshire, England.

Glow in the dark

There's said to be a glowing light around the body of every living person. This was discovered in the 1930s by Russian professor Semyan Kirlian who took photographs that showed sparks of light coming from people's bodies.

The Black Cat of KILLAKEE

Over the centuries, cats have been linked to mysterious happenings. When a cat arches its back and hisses, it's because it has seen a ghost. As for the Black Cat of Killakee, it was a ghost itself.

At long last, the old house in the village of Killakee, Ireland, was being repaired. It had stood empty for many years, and locals said that it was haunted by the ghost of a giant cat.

There were rumors that the old house at Killakee was haunted—but this didn't put the builders off.

One day in 1968, the door to the house was found open, and when a workman went inside he found a ghostly black cat as big as a dog staring at him through blood-red eyes.

The cat was bigger than a normal cat, and its eyes were the color of blood.

Long-lost cats

The dried-out mummified bodies of cats are sometimes found inside old buildings in Europe. It was believed that cats brought good luck, so builders hid cats behind walls and under floorboards, thinking they would protect the house.

This was just the start. Over the coming weeks, the house echoed to the sound of knocks and bangs, vases were smashed, and pictures fell from the walls, as if a poltergeist was present. It was all too much for Margaret O'Brien, the owner, who asked a priest to rid the house of the harmful spirit. The priest did this and all was well.

27

Hunting for GHOSTS

Science became involved with ghost hunting when the first photographs of ghostly shapes were taken. Today's ghost hunters set cameras running, equipped with lenses that can see in the dark.

Loyd Auerback of JFK University, California conducts field investigations of paranormal activity, using photographic equipment.

INVESTIGATING THE SCENE

Other devices look for sudden falls in the temperature, since it's thought this indicates a ghostly presence. Eyewitnesses are interviewed, facts are checked and double-checked, and a description slowly emerges. It's like police work, investigating the scene of a crime.

FINDING AN EXPLANATION

When ghost hunters begin looking into a new case, they know they might find nothing unusual. Perhaps they find that a knocking noise can be explained by a loose pipe. A ghost photograph might turn out to be the result of a faulty camera.

It's been calculated that 98 percent of all ghost stories can be given everyday explanations. That leaves 2 percent that can't be explained. It's these rare cases that might just prove that ghosts really do exist.

An investigation team measure the presence of electricity in the ground of a cemetery. They believe that this might show paranormal activity.

Harry Price, Ghost Hunter

Harry Price (1881–1948) was a famous ghost hunter from England. In the 1920s, he started using scientific methods to look for ghosts. He set up a laboratory where he carried out experiments. Price also investigated haunted places, and wrote several books about his findings.

TIMELINE

1537 Janet Douglas was burned at the stake. Her ghost is said to haunt Glamis Castle, Scotland, U.K., and is known as the Grey Lady.

1817 A poltergeist known as the Bell Witch pestered the Bell family in Robertson for four years.

1843 The ghost story *A Christmas Carol*, by Charles Dickens, was published.

1848 Maggie and Kate Fox, of Hydesville claimed they could communicate with the spirit world.

1863 Borley Rectory was built, and became notorious as the most haunted house in England. It was destroyed by fire in 1939.

1901 Charlotte Moberly and Eleanor Jourdain believed they had seen the ghost of Queen Marie Antionette, at Versailles, France.

1920s Harry Price began his work as a ghost hunter in England.

1936 The Brown Lady photograph was taken, at Raynham Hall, Norfolk, England. It is one of the most famous ghost photographs ever taken.

1939 *The Friendly Ghost*, a book for children, was published. It featured a ghost called Casper.

1975 George and Kathleen Lutz claimed their house in Amityville was haunted. A book and movie were made about the events.

1984 The movie *Ghostbusters* was released.

Ghostbusters was about a team of ghost catchers in New York City.

BILL MURRAY   DAN AYKROYD
SIGOURNEY WEAVER
GH STBUSTERS

2008 A photograph taken at Tantallon Castle, Scotland, seems to show a figure of a woman in Tudor clothes.

GLOSSARY

CYCLICAL GHOST

A type of ghsot that appears in the same place again and again.

DOPPELGANGER

A type of ghost. It means "double-walker" and is the ghostly double of a person who is still alive.

GHOST

The image of a person, an animal, or a thing such as a ship that is not really there.

HOAX

Something that is made up on purpose, and is meant to make people believe it is real.

MEDIUM

A person who claims they can contact the dead.

ORB

A ball of light that can only be seen with a camera, and which is claimed to be a form of ghostly energy.

POLTERGEIST

A type of ghost. It moves objects, causes fires, and makes noises.

PSYCHIC

A person who claims they can read minds and perform other mysterious actions.

PSYCHOKINESIS

The power to make an object move just by thinking about it.

SEANCE

A meeting at which people work with a medium to contact the dead.

SPIRIT

Another word for a ghost. It can also mean a person's soul.

TIME SLIP

The feeling that time has somehow changed from the present day to the past.

INDEX